Th

'*The Wilderness* is essentially a simple story, of thwarted passions, frustrated ambitions and hunger for land, but in the hands of O'Flaherty it becomes a tour de force that tears through the mind with the careless abandon of an Atlantic breaker.'

Sunday Press

The Black Soul

'Embodies an energy that is genius.'

W.B. Yeats

'An elemental book because the primitive passions run free.'

AE

Famine

'A major achievement — a masterpiece. The kind of truth only a major writer of fiction is capable of portraying.'

Anthony Burgess

'The author's skill as a storyteller is at times breathtaking. This is a most rewarding novel.'

Publishers Weekly

'A marvellously visual writer who prints his description on the retina.'

The Guardian

Skerrett

'One of the most powerful novels that this master-writer has ever produced.'

The Irish Times

'Liam O'Flaherty is a great, great writer whose work must be unique in any language, any culture. He has all the potential for becoming a matrix for the yearnings of another generation.'

Neil Jordan

'Powerful in language, majestic in scope, utterly honest.'

Sunday Press

LIAM O'FLAHERTY

Born in 1896 on Inishmore, the largest of the Aran Islands, Liam O'Flaherty grew up in a world of awesome beauty, echoes from his descendants and the ancient pagan past. From his father, a Fenian, O'Flaherty inherited a rebellious streak; from his mother, a noted *seanchaí*, came the deep spiritualism and love of nature that has enraptured readers through the decades.

In France in 1917, O'Flaherty was severely shell-shocked. After a short recuperation, he spent several restless years travelling the globe. In 1920 he supported the Republican cause against the Free State government. Influenced by the Industrial Workers of the World's programme of social revolution, O'Flaherty organised the seizure and occupation of the Rotunda Theatre at the top of Dublin's O'Connell Street in 1922. He hoisted the red flag of revolution, calling himself the 'Chairman of the Council of the Unemployed', but fled three days later to avoid bloodshed. Later that year he moved to London, where his writing skills came to the attention of critic Edward Garnett, who recommended to Jonathan Cape the publication of O'Flaherty's first novel. For the next two decades, O'Flaherty's creative output was astonishing. Writing in English and Irish, he produced novels, memoirs and short stories by the dozen. Remarkable for their literary value and entertainment, O'Flaherty's books are also crucial from an anthropological point of view, charting the ways and beliefs of a peasant world before it was eclipsed by modernity.

Some of O'Flaherty's work was banned in Ireland — he was a rebel in his writing, as in his life. Liam O'Flaherty died in Dublin in 1984, aged 88 years, having enriched forever Irish literature and culture.

Other books by LIAM O'FLAHERTY
available from WOLFHOUND PRESS

FICTION
Famine
Short Stories: The Pedlar's Revenge
The Wilderness
Skerrett
Insurrection
The Assassin
The Ecstasy of Angus
Thy Neighbour's Wife
The Black Soul
The Informer
Return of the Brute
Mr Gilhooley

AUTOBIOGRAPHY
Shame the Devil

FOR CHILDREN
The Test of Courage
All Things Come of Age

OTHER
The Letters of Liam O'Flaherty
(Edited by A.A. Kelly)

FORTHCOMING
The Collected Stories of Liam O'Flaherty

LIAM O'FLAHERTY
A Tourist's Guide to Ireland

WOLFHOUND PRESS
& in the US and Canada
The Irish American Book Company

This edition published in 1998 by
Wolfhound Press Ltd
68 Mountjoy Square
Dublin 1, Ireland
Tel: (353-1) 874 0354
Fax: (353-1) 872 0207

Published in the US and Canada by
The Irish American Book Company
6309 Monarch Park Place
Niwot, Colorado 80503, USA
Tel: (303) 652-2710
Fax: (303) 652-2689

© 1929, 1998 Liam O'Flaherty
First edition London, 1929

All rights reserved. No part of this book may be reproduced or utilised in any form or by any means digital, electronic or mechanical including photography, filming, video recording, photocopying, or by any information storage and retrieval system or shall not, by way of trade or otherwise, be lent, resold or otherwise circulated in any form of binding or cover other than that in which it is published without prior permission in writing from the publisher.

Wolfhound Press receives financial assistance from the Arts Council/ An Chomhairle Ealaíon, Dublin.

British Library Cataloguing in Publication Data
A catalogue record for this book is available from the British Library.

ISBN 0-86327-589-3

10 9 8 7 6 5 4 3 2 1

Cover image based on a photograph by Peter Zoeller
Cover Design: Slick Fish Design
Typesetting: Wolfhound Press
Printed and bound by The Guernsey Press Co. Ltd, Guernsey, Channel Islands

~ *One* ~

The tourist is at the mercy of every kind of ruffian. Although every country holds out welcoming hands to him, it is only for the purpose of robbing him of all he possesses, and if he is caught escaping, at the end of his holiday, with even a small silver coin in his pockets, it's more than likely that the Customs officers are going to fine him to that amount for taking away on his shoes some of the country's mud. And yet, even though the tourist is mulcted in this scandalous manner, in every country, he is always looked upon as a low fellow, an inquisitive, vulgar beggar, a loud-mouthed trot-about, a coarse eater, a foreigner. There are jokes in every literature about his capacity for snoring, about his clothes and about his wife, who seems to be always either very fat or very skinny.

Now, why is this? I have come to the conclusion that it all results from the tourist being ignorant of the countries into which he goes for a visit. True enough, he is provided by the railways and by the tourist agencies with a great deal of information, but very little of it is credible except by a gullible and excitable person like a tourist. Information is scattered broadcast, on handbills, in newspapers, on posters produced by artists who should have more respect for their art than prostituting it to the service of such sharp practices (to put it nicely). But this information concerns itself solely with the geographical nature of the country, with hotels and railways and such things. Information as to the character and habits of the *people* is never given, at least to my knowledge.

Yet this is the information that is most necessary. For to know the habits and character of one's enemy is to be able to over-reach him at his own game of exploitation. Therefore, as I am an honest man and am not connected with the *Tourist Industry*, I propose to save the tourist, at least in this country. And as I suppose all countries, as far as robbing the tourist is concerned, are more or less alike, I'll save him in every country too. And, mark you, by doing this, I'll also confer a benefit on the *Tourist Industry*. For, since the tourist in future will come to Ireland impregnable within the armour provided by my information, he'll come without fear and in great numbers. In this manner the *Industry* will benefit, as by a greater turnover of small profits it will gather a greater income than by its former method of looting the few without shame or conscience.

How many kinds of tourists are there? Obviously there are a great many kinds of tourists, a myriad. But they may safely be divided into four main classes, those who come for knowledge, those who come for pleasure, those who come for a rest and those who

One

come for profit. This last class is a small one, composed of robbers, swindlers, shysters and confidence tricksters. As I have no respect for these people, I'll leave them to the mercy of the Irish *Tourist Industry*. It's a very fitting punishment. I therefore dismiss this class and I propose to deal solely with the remaining three classes.

Having examined and classified the tourists, it is now necessary to examine and classify the Irish people, or such of them as come into conflict with the tourist. I think, as far as the Irish people are concerned, it will be necessary to study the priests, the politicians, the publicans and the peasants. I omit the hotel-keepers, the garage proprietors, the shop-keepers, the dairymen and the boarding house keepers, because in every country these types openly fly the flag of commercial piracy and even the most ignorant tourist will not fail to recognise them and to beware of them. However, if I discover, in my examination, any particular local eccentricity, I am going to set it down.

~ *Two* ~

No doubt the tourist will have heard, long before his arrival in this country, that Ireland was once known as the island of saints and scholars. Every tourist worth his salt knows this, for the tourist is noted for his catch-cries and his ingenuous belief that by uttering these cries he is going to impress the natives by his knowledge of their history, their habits and their virtues. Here, I must warn the tourist against making any reference to Ireland as the island of saints and scholars. Nobody in Ireland nowadays believes that legend and the well-meaning tourist giving voice to it will be suspected of trying to give offence. If the tourist wishes to show his interest in the religion or learning of the country and thereby ingratiate himself, he may remark casually: 'Well! I suppose there are as many priests in Ireland as when my father was here forty years ago?' And the reply will be, gloomily or proudly, as the case may be: 'As many as ever.'

That reply will be a true one. The priests are as numerous as ever they were, and perhaps even more numerous, if that were possible. Whether their existence, and in such numbers, is to the benefit of the country does not concern me here, as this book is for the enlightenment of the tourist. And as the tourist does not have to live in this country, one cannot expect him to be interested in its welfare. Therefore, as impartially as possible, I propose to examine that numerous and respectable class of our community, the priests.

There have been priests in Ireland for thousands of years. Indeed, the island was very probably discovered by a priest or priests, who, noticing that the configuration of the country and the climate were remarkably adapted towards producing mystical inclinations, brought hither some lay followers to act as the nucleus of a congregation. Nobody knows the name of the religion exploited by those first priests, and even their God is long since deceased. In fact, numbers of Gods and religions have found followers and emoluments and temples in this country since then and have disappeared again, leaving no trace, other than the fairies, which are worshipped in mountainy places by incurably conservative peasants. But even though the Gods and the religions change and disappear, the priests remain, always the same; and to my mind they seem to get sturdier and fatter as the centuries pass.

The religion at present authorised by the priests is the Christian religion. It has been in vogue for something like two thousand years and is still very flourishing, without any sign of a rival. When I say there is no rival to the Christian religion in this country I mean that no other religion has officiating priests, and

Two

without priests no religion can be considered seriously. It has no backbone and no real terror. The various tribes of fairies that are so esteemed by remote peasants and by some of the old-fashioned poets of the last generation are merely very charming spirits. Nobody pays them any material respect by the building of temples or the sprinkling of holy water, and although W.B. Yeats and George Russell, and others, have written poetry in their honour, these poems have had no result whatsoever in changing the allegiance of the priests. I would earnestly warn all tourists against having any truck with fairies or with those that boost fairies. Any tourist who meddles with them will only succeed in antagonising the priests. And that would be very dangerous.

The power of the priests in Ireland has always been very great, and it is still as great as ever. Those foolish people who say that the priests are losing their power make, in my opinion, a great mistake. Whenever the priests appear to be losing power it merely means that they are changing their outward appearance. When the Druids, a former dynasty of priests, gave way to the Christian hermits they merely transformed themselves into Christians. How they did this I know not. They may have changed themselves into spirits and flown down the throats of the Christians. Whatever happened, it is certain that the priests nowadays have all the characteristics of the Druids. They merely worship a different God. In the same manner the priests of the present day may change into some other dynasty of priests, but the tourist may be sure that they have no intention of losing their power. Because, as long as the

A Tourist's Guide to Ireland

Irish climate remains what it is and the Irish mountains bring mist and fog, there will always be a vast proportion of the population under the influence of mystical dreams and mystical terrors. And to counteract these terrors and dreams priests are absolutely necessary. So let the tourist beware of toying with any new-fangled notions that the priests may be scoffed at with impunity. Let him beware of Dublin drawing-rooms, where it is now fashionable to preach liberalism and to refer to the priests as the cause of the country's ignorance, poverty and apathy. Although it may be true that the priests are the cause of all this, the fact remains that it is not safe to say so in a country district. Let the tourist carefully note this.

Let him be a sane man. He is bound to go into a country district if he wants to see Ireland, and if he goes into a country district, he cannot avoid coming in contact with the local priests. If he follows my advice, he will act as follows.

In each parish there are two or three priests. One is a parish priest. The others, if there are two, are curates. The tourist need pay no attention to the curates. They have no power as far as the tourist is concerned. If a tourist is a woman, however, she may interest herself in the curates. Some of them are very spiritual, and have been known to inspire women of a certain type with passions of a very refined sort. But for the male tourist, the curates are of no account. They are very poor. They are under the thumb of their parish priest. They are merely priests in training. On the other hand, the parish priest must be carefully studied and, where possible, exploited.

Two

On arriving in a country district, unless the tourist has already made arrangements for his hotel, he should make subtle inquiries before choosing a hotel. There may be several hotels or boarding houses in the district. He should therefore endeavour to find out if the parish priest has an interest in any particular one. It is more than likely that he has, financial or otherwise. Having discovered which is the parish priest's hotel, the tourist should go to it.

This may seem extraordinary, but it is true that in remote parts of Ireland, usually the parts of interest to tourists, the parish priest has a finger in every pie. He is the great and only power in the district. Confident in the blind worship of the peasants and the village loafers and the fishermen of the seaside, he forces the wealthier people to obey him in the most minute matters. He is practically master of the body and soul of every individual. When they are born they are brought before him and he baptises them for a few shillings. When they begin to go to school they come under his supervision. He hires and sacks their teachers at his discretion, very often at his whim. He flogs them if they mitch from school or if they fail to learn their catechism. When they become striplings he watches them carefully lest they make love clandestinely. When they reach marriageable age he marries them for a few pounds. If they don't get married he nags at them, eager for his fees. He abuses them from the altar unless they pay him what he considers sufficient money at Christmas and Easter. When they die he buries them, but before doing so, he levies a further toll in hard cash over their dead bodies. This toll is levied from all their relatives.

From their first yell at birth until the sod falls on them in their grave their actions and thoughts are under his direction. He is, almost invariably, himself of peasant abstraction and almost invariably he is just about as well informed as a well-informed peasant. So he is not burthened by a very refined religious conscience in the civilised sense of the word. Being mentally on a level with his peasant flock, he is up to all their tricks. He knows what is passing in their minds, of what they are afraid, how to tickle their greed, how to overawe them with threats of hell, or to enthuse them with promises of indulgences and eternal happiness . So they are proud of him, as of something that has sprung from their loins, that satisfies their innate greed by giving a promise of Heaven and that is just a little cleverer than themselves. Not too clever, for too much cleverness inspires a peasant with distrust.

This sense of power leads the parish priest inevitably into the commission of various excesses which may be of interest to the tourist and which may very well redound to his benefit. Finding himself in the position of a dictator, the parish priest usually assumes the manners of a parvenu aristocrat. As the aristocracy has been wiped out during the tumults of the past couple of generations, he has no competitors. And it is in the character of the lord of the manor that he is vulnerable at the hands of the subtle tourist.

Having installed himself in the parish priest's hotel, the wise tourist makes the acquaintance of the parish

Two

priest. The best form of introduction is a small donation of about five pounds for a charitable cause. There is bound to be one in the pocket of every parish priest. It is either a church that is being built or a church that is being mended or some poor family that has lost its bread-winner. Sometimes it may be one of the good priest's relatives that needs a place or a dot, but the tourist must not be too inquisitive. He is merely to hand over his few pounds as quietly as possible, and the trick is done. He'll get much more in return than the value of his money. For, once he has been admitted to the parish priest's house as a guest he is received in the district as one of the people. The tradesmen no longer dare rob him, and if his motor car breaks down, due to some slight defect, the garage proprietor will not dare tamper with the engine in order to get further custom. If he has no motor car and wants to take a ride on an Irish jaunting car to visit some ruin, he is accompanied by the parish priest, and the only expense will be probably a *pour boire* for the driver and a few coppers for the stray children that are peeping from behind ditches. He may take a boat on the lake or on the sea and fish to his heart's content and the parish priest's mandate insures him against the usual extortion. Old men, hearing that he is the priest's friend, are quite content to tell him the usual stories, ones that were first invented to amuse people like Lady Gregory, without suggesting at the end of their recitation that their pipes are without tobacco. The local sergeant of police will look the other way when the tourist wants a drink after hours and if he is seen flirting with a pretty girl of the locality, the parish fanatic will not dare send a scurrilous letter to the Authorities in Dublin. In fact, the wise tourist can enjoy himself immensely for five or ten pounds. He'll enjoy seeing his fellow tourists being mulcted right and left by the shark of a hotel proprietor, while he himself is treated to all kinds of luxuries, with the assurance, from the parish priest, that it will not cost anything extra and that the bill is going to be moderate. At the same time, if he wants to do so, he may dine every day at the parish priest's house and drink as much whiskey, licit and illicit, as he likes.

These dinners at the parish priest's house are well worth any tourist's trouble, and if the business of attracting the tourist were taken over by the Government instead of being left to the mercy of the hotel people, the parish priest's dinner would stand out as Ireland's great delicacy on all the advertisement hoardings of the world. It is not a modern meal in the French manner, with a great deal of sauce and suspicion. It is a plain business, above board, without any doubt as to the authenticity of the beef or fish. The only thing that is old is the whiskey. Everything is in vast quantity. The parish priest himself does the carving, and he stands up to whet his knife, which he brandishes like a Chinese headsman. Appetite is whetted by the sight of such abundance, and it is goaded to excess by the exhortations of the parish priest, who sees in the dinner the culminating point of the scheme which has caused all this hospitality.

For there is a scheme and the tourist must be warned of it. Without due warning he is a helpless

Two

victim at the end of the meal. For his unsolicited donation will have persuaded the parish priest that he is both rich and foolish and a man to be exploited. In return for this feasting the parish priest expects to be able to put the tourist on his list of donators for the rest of his life. For this reason it is absolutely necessary for the tourist to conceal his address. Otherwise the parish priest will pester him with letters and it is useless to try and ignore these letters. They are quite able to draw blood out a turnip. On the other hand, if the tourist is a subtle fellow, after my own heart, he will give a false address and then go away laughing to himself, after having done what no man has yet done, having got something for nothing out of a parish priest.

Of course, I must also warn the tourist that there are some parish priests who are too much of a handful for even the most subtle tourist. These are of the thin, furtive type. They have small eyes and they are nervous in their movements up to a great age. They hover about the railway stations and the steamboat landing places, and they fix their eyes on every stranger, with the searching glance of a detective. Nothing escapes them. They know everything. Their servants are thin and so are their horses. They argue over their petty bills. Their village beggars are ragged and hollow-cheeked. Their school teachers have a haunted look. Even in the most remote district the police sergeant wears his uniform every day, when under the observation of one of those gentlemen. They are no good to anybody, least of all to the tourist, and the tourist must avoid them like a plague. For they have all the shame-

A Tourist's Guide to Ireland

lessness of the miser, and are quite prepared to use threats and insults, and even to go down on their knees in order to extract money out of the tourist's pockets.

But when the tourist sees that the parish priest is fat and jovial and owns a good horse and wears riding breeches and goes around everywhere with a horsewhip, then he should go ahead. That type of parish priest has a good disposition, and he is a man of the world and, as far as the subtle tourist is concerned, a fool.

The tourist must also know what to say to the parish priest. He should on no account be drawn into a discussion of any religious matter. For the parish priest has no great interest in religion. It is his business, and a very private one, and as he does not know very much about the philosophy of religion, he prefers to make a mystery of it. Neither must the tourist refer to books or to art of any description. The parish priest dislikes books, except a few books which it would be tiresome for the tourist to read. But the tourist may casually refer to Canon Sheehan as the greatest novelist the world has ever produced. Try to remember the name *Canon Sheehan*. There is no need to learn by rote the names of his books because the parish priest is likely to be ignorant of them himself. Apart from this reference to *Canon Sheehan*, literature must not be mentioned on any account. And if the tourist is taken around the parish church, he must not try to be polite by referring to the statues or the pictures as works of art. Of course they are sure to be monstrosities, but a tourist is quite capable of telling any lie in order to ingratiate himself. To a

Two

parish priest, the St Francis of El Greco is just a Holy Picture and must be referred to as such. Other than Holy Pictures the only pictures that may be referred to are the photographs in the daily newspapers. Neither must education be discussed. The parish priest regards any references by a layman to education as a sign of Free Masonry. No form of amusement must be discussed, except after a long intimacy, which, in itself, is to be avoided. For the parish priest regards any form of amusement as irreligious and dangerous to faith and morals.

In fact, there are only two forms of conversation allowed. They are politics and gossip. Gossip may concern itself with scandalous stories about people who are not Catholics. These scandalous stories may be as obscene as possible, but always told in a gloomy voice. The parish priest himself is bound to have a store, which he is quite eager to untap.

Politics must also be approached in a subtle way. The conversation should open on the part of the tourist by a pathetic reference to the deplorable state of the country, due to inability of the politicians to establish some sort of a common agreement that would stop the younger generation in its mad career to material and moral ruin. The evils of all-night dancing and reading English Sunday newspapers should be vaguely attributed to the lack of a common understanding among the politicians. That is non-committal and is quite sufficient to set the parish priest in motion. The tourist need say no more. He may nod his head occasionally in agreement, or strike the table or empty his glass at the precise moment when the parish priest is stressing some point with particular violence. He must restrain his laughter or his amazement, and if he has scruples about morals he should do his best to hide his indignation. For indeed, my tourist must be very subtle if he successfully undergoes this test of listening calmly to a parish priest giving his views on politics.

In fact, properly speaking, no parish priest has any convictions on politics. At the back of his mind, he regards the state as an enemy that has usurped the temporal power of the Pope. Being an enemy, the state must be exploited as much as possible and without any qualms of conscience. Because of this innate and perhaps unconscious hostility to the state as an institution, the parish priest cannot see that it is the duty of a citizen to endeavour to make political life as morally clean as possible. He cannot see that the community as a whole must always come into the forefront of every citizen's political consciousness and that personal interests must be sacrificed to the interests of the nation. No. The parish priest regards himself as the commander of his parish, which he is holding for His Majesty the Pope. Between himself and the Pope there is the Bishop, acting, so to speak, as the Divisional Commander. As far as the Civil Power is concerned, it is a semi-hostile force which must be kept in check, kept in tow, intrigued against and exploited, until that glorious day when the Vicar of Christ again is restored to his proper position as the ruler of the earth and the wearer of the Imperial Crown.

This point of view helps the parish priest to adopt a

Two

very cold-blooded attitude towards Irish politics. He is merely either for or against the government. If he has a relative in a government position, he is in favour of the government. If he has a relative who wants a position and cannot get it, then he is against the government. But his support of the government is very precarious and he makes many visits to Dublin and creeps up back stairs into ministerial offices, cajoling and threatening. He is most commonly seen making a cautious approach to the Education Office, where he has all sorts of complaints to lodge and all sorts of suggestions to make. Every book recommended by the education authorities for the schools is examined by him, and if he finds a single idea in any of them that might be likely to inspire thought of passion, then he is up in arms at once. Like an army of black beetles on the march, he and his countless brothers invade Dublin and lay siege to the official responsible. Woe to that man.

Woe to them all, all the ministers and responsible officials. For our parish priest has an interest in everything. For every public position they have their candidates. In every representative body they are present, either as Chairmen or Honorary Presidents, and they keep a stern eye on everybody. To be accused by a parish priest in one of these assemblies as a man of revolutionary or unchaste sentiments is to suffer social extermination. And even in parliament, where the parish priest is refused admission as a member, the hapless members feel themselves under the same supervision. Every word they utter, every move they make reaches the ears of the parish priest, and when the next election comes, if they have erred, they are thrust out into the darkness.

As he is thus a sort of grand master of a secret society, the parish priest abhors rival secret societies. He always denounces them and he really fears them. Free Masons, Communists, Liberals, and even such harmless people as members of the Frothblowers, come under his displeasure. As for the Fenians, who believe in armed revolt and the establishment of a militant republic, he loathes them. For he sees in all these societies and ideas a tendency towards strengthening the power of the state and robbing the confessional of some of its terrors.

He has an idea that Ireland is the only moral country in the world. And yet his personal view of the Irish people as individuals is a very poor one. He is firmly convinced that the English people are immoral, principally on the score of lechery. The French are even worse. The Americans are very doubtful people, on account of the facility for divorce in that country. Germany is not so bad, because Bavaria is a Catholic country. The Russians are altogether beyond the pale of civilisation as they have nationalised women and overthrown the Church. The Italians, Spaniards and Belgians are very nearly as pure as the Irish. The Chinese are rather bad, but there is great hope for them, on account of the Irish Mission to China, for which he may touch the tourist, if he (the parish priest) has a relative in that organisation. The Mexicans are even worse than the Russians and he spends his spare time intriguing with newspapers and politicians in order to get Ireland

Two

to get England to get America to make war on Mexico.

This conversation and these extraordinary views will first inspire the tourist, if he is an educated man interested in the progress of civilisation and culture, with disgust. But on second thought, after he has taken a walk by the sea shore or along the mountain slope in the moonlight and digested his heavy dinner and scattered the fumes of his whiskey, he will begin to see the parish priest in a correct perspective. Then he will understand, if he is kindly, as I hope he is, that the parish priest is not a monster or an evil genius, but a poor grown-up child who is the victim of his environment. He errs through crass ignorance rather than through a natural predestination towards evil. As a rule he is a kindly soul, and if he is a harsh tyrant of manners and social activities, it is the forgivable tyranny of the big boy in the village school who is more fond of showing his muscle than of giving pain through a love of pain in itself. The parish priest himself has had no education worth speaking of, so he dislikes others receiving one. His training in the seminary has been one of unhealthy suppression of all natural inclination, so his simple mind is convinced that all men must be lashed with scorpions and clothed in sack when the little pretty devil of the flesh shows its frolicsome head. Himself born in poverty and forbidden by his Divine Master to accumulate wealth, he gets rich furtively like Père Grandet and the secrecy of his penny-gathering inspires him with the distrust, the glowering eye and the dreadful yellow lust of the miser. He is hemmed in on all sides by fetishes and dogmas, so that his crude mind, which was destined by nature to understand no more than the mechanism of the plough and the habits of the plodding horse, is forced to undergo a continuous travail in the unravelling of his cupidity from the meshes of his religion.

Finally, he is forced by the priestly law of celibacy to remain a savage to the end of his days. For all men that are cut off from the gentle companionship and the refining influence of women are perforce savages. Their corrupted and unscattered seed grows within them like a foul weed poisoning the growth and flowering of all healthy passions. Their gift of life is brought by them to the grave and they refuse to hand it on to some lovely child that would grow about their withering thighs and charm their old eyes with an image of their youth. Let the tourist then pity them and forget the passing evil of their minds. Let him even feel a little ashamed of having exploited them as he goes away.

But here ... No more sentiment. The tourist must stand fast. He has been robbed too often. And no man can feel so capable of fine feeling as he who has been often robbed and has robbed in return. After revenge comes reconciliation.

However, I have no doubt but that among the many kinds of tourists, there is going to be an Englishman of the idealistic type who insists on getting to the bottom of every social evil that he comes across and then tries to remedy it. That type of Englishman is as obstinate as a mule, and there is no use in my appealing to him to go away quietly, after he has investigated my parish priest. He will consider himself in duty bound to make

Two

a thorough investigation of the whole order of the priesthood and very probably he'll leave the country hot with passion, which may lead him to write a letter to *The Times*, or, indeed, to write a book entitled, perhaps, *Clericalism in Ireland and Its Effects on the Social Organism*, with a sub-title *Being The Result of a Fortnight's Careful Study of the Growth of Church Property in Ireland. Together with Some Thoughts on the Lack of Personal Initiative among the Populace Caused by the Evils of Clerical Control of All Branches of Social Activity.*

Lest the idealistic tourist may commit any indiscretion owing to the heat of his passion and the limited time at his disposal for investigation, I think I am in duty bound to give him a general outline of the method in which such a work should be approached so that a fair result may be achieved .

The idealist must understand before proceeding to study the priesthood as a whole that it is quite a hopeless task. For the organisation is directed from Rome and he cannot obtain admission to the archives of the Sacred College. He may wander around Ireland and note different classes of priests with different activities, but he will be at a loss where to begin to study them. For like a worm, it will be very difficult to distinguish the head from the tail. To the ordinary unsophisticated individual, the barbarian or the non-Catholic, the Cardinal seems to be the head. But that is utterly false. The Cardinal is merely the Officer Commanding the infantry. The Bishops are Colonels Commanding Battalions. The Canons are the Company Captains. The Parish Priests are the hefty Sergeant-majors. The Curates are the Corporals who do all the routine work. Just as the British Army is based on the efficiency of the sergeant-major and the corporal, so is the army of priests. But without that wise body of thinkers at the War Office, the tacticians, the propagandists and the intelligence officers, the British Army would be a rather futile mechanism of brawn and swear words, and courage and beer. In the same way, the army of priests would be entirely ineffectual without the Religious Orders.

Just as the parish priest is a stupid, good-natured sort of village tyrant, so is the religious priest the exact opposite. He is almost invariably an educated man. He is subtle, refined and as a general rule ascetic. Living within a college or monastery, he practises a certain very definite form of Christianity and thus inspires the laity with respect and the parish priests with envy. In fact, the parish priest always thinks and speaks of the regular priest in the same manner as the fighting soldier thinks and speaks of the Brass Hat. Yet, if the priesthood is an evil in this country, the religious priest is more responsible than the parish priest, in spite of his shy ways, his refinement and asceticism. But how is he an evil to the tourist? That is the point. If he is not an evil to the tourist he is not an evil at all, and he does not concern us; for I am already sick of my friend, the idealist, and I have come to the conclusion that he deserves no assistance in the concoction of his horrible book with the atrocious sub-titles. I hope the Jesuits catch him at it.

Yes ... the Jesuits. Let us begin with the Jesuits. Are the Jesuits then culpable of robbing the tourist? They

Two

are, because they rob him of pleasure. For every tourist understands how pleasant it is to go into a country where the middle classes are well informed, energetic, urbane, cultured, and with a high standard of social morality; where those pleasures which are fostered by the middle classes in all countries are everywhere to be tasted: music, the theatre, the cabaret, the all-night café, and perhaps delicate facilities for the more choice kinds of amorous affairs. These pleasures, alas, are at a discount in our country owing to the strange disease that has fastened on our priesthood since the Jesuits set the tone and the pace of national education. For in this land where the Gael was once noted above all the races of the earth 'for beauty and lasciviousness' (to quote an ancient poet), the heavy, hairy garment of Puritanism has fallen and enshrouded the whole of society. Laughter, that music most sweet of all human music, the gift of Dionysian wine, is seldom heard, for the lamentations of the damned are extolled by the Jesuits as the only fitting cry for an unfortunate human being. The drinking feasts of Fionn and his gallant roysterers have given place to secretive sousings in dirty public houses, where no female dare enter, unless she be clothed in rags and bleary in the eye. Here, where the poets once received a herd of cattle for a poem, the divine fire of song in the eye is as hateful as the gleam in the eye of a courtesan. To be a poet is to be an anti-Christ, unless it be the drivelling doggerel composed over the death of a Papal Potentate. The theatre, except for the solitary exception of the Abbey Theatre, is left in the hands of 'the lecherous English,' as being suitable solely for that 'immoral race.' It is as difficult to get a licence for a cabaret as it is to grow a pine tree on the Aran Islands. All this is due to the Jesuits and to their fellow-workers, the members of the numerous other religious orders.

Just as the secular clergy control primary education, secondary education is in the hands of the religious clergy, principally in the hands of the Jesuits. As the parish priest moulds the mind of the peasant, of the small town idler, of the fisherman and of the cattle drover, the Jesuit moulds the mind of the middle class citizen. And the result is that the middle class citizen is generally much less intelligent than the peasant. For the peasant has the earth, the sea and nature to wash his mind with, clearing away much of the drivel that he has learned at school, whereas the middle class citizen has no such opportunities. Rather he is confounded at every step in his career by the antagonism between the teaching of the Jesuits and the accumulated knowledge of the other countries where Jesuits have not throttled human culture with the tanned noose of dogma. Being confounded in this manner, he becomes a confounded nuisance to every clear thinking person. He allows himself, even when fully grown and perhaps bearded, to be herded into organisations called confraternities and Catholic Truth Societies, and swashbuckling organisations whose purpose is the militant overthrow of everything that is not pleasant to the minds of the Jesuits. The Jesuits, being subtle and educated men, never use their muscles like the parish priests, but utter frozen words after the manner of Rabelais, and sending out these words into the minds of their subjects prevail upon their subjects to do their bidding. Like those monks in Rabelais that were fed upon wind, our middle class citizens are so bloated by this unhealthy sort of feeding that they are absolute fanatics on certain matters. And the tourist must treat them very gently, lest on the least provocation they belch forth hurricanes of fanaticism that might blow the tourist across the ocean to the farthest confines of the western world.

The Jesuits are also the propagandists of the Church. In this capacity they carry on campaigns in the newspapers. They publish periodicals and they prevent free-thinking citizens from publishing periodicals that challenge their concept of the universe. Although without legal authority, so great is their power that no group of free-thinking citizens dare band together for the purpose of producing a periodical that is manifestly non-Christian or purely intellectual. On the rare occasions when groups of citizens have tried to publish periodicals of that sort these periodicals have come to a sudden end. For this reason, the tourist desirous of finding out what the intellectuals of the country are thinking and doing will have to run from one drawing-room to another and from one public house to another and from one studio to another, instead of going to the news shops as in other countries where there is freedom of intellectual expression. As a matter of fact, if he really wants to find out what the chief intellectuals of Ireland are thinking he'll have to go abroad to England, America and to Paris, where the author of *Ulysses* is living in exile. He will search the Irish newspapers for any sign of intellectual life and he will find none, and if he is an educated man, used to the amenities of a cultured life, he will find it very tiring to be forced to adopt ancient methods of satisfying the craving of his soul, the method of conversation, practically in secret. His sense of dignity will be offended by the sight of penniless scholars and of all culture being held in suspicion and treated with contumely.

He'll see other orders of religious clergy who make it their business to go around the country on missions terrorising the unfortunate lower classes with threats of fire and brimstone in the hereafter, while in their train march countless vendors of statues, medals, scapulars and *agnus deis*, which are used by the ignorant in the place of medicine. He'll find other orders that live simply by begging. And on every side, among all orders, he'll find a rapid accumulation of property, which threatens to turn the whole country into a clerical kingdom. He'll meet nuns, also accumulating property. He'll meet Christian Brothers, who are in the teaching business, midway between the secular clergy and the religious orders. And he'll finish up, if he is any way sensitive, by getting an impression of Ireland, as a beautiful sad-faced country that is being rapidly covered by a black rash.

~ *Three* ~

Next to priests, the politicians are easily the most important class of the Irish community. It is very difficult to estimate whether they are enemies or friends of the tourist. They give him a great deal of pleasure and amusement, but at the same time they cost him a lot of money. It he is rich he will not mind the money, and he will know that nowadays it is not everywhere that amusement can be found. The rich have been moaning for thousands of years that the genius of man is capable of inventing everything but a new vice. We in Ireland may not be able to claim the invention of a distinctly new vice, but our politicians have undoubtedly made the vice of politics much more interesting than it is in other countries.

Of course, the tourist, being here only for a short period, cannot indulge in this vice by actual participation, but he can watch it. If he listens to me carefully, he'll know how to set about watching it, where to get in touch with the more interesting types of addicts and when to come to the country if he gets enthusiastic and wishes to see this vice rampant.

We have seen in our study of the priests that the art of conversation is the only one recognised by the priests. This breeds a veritable passion for talking among us. The tourist wandering in lonely country districts may chance to see two peasants standing in adjacent fields, at a considerable distance from one another. Each may have a plough or a spade, but neither is paying any attention to his tool. They are both talking in a loud voice. And if the tourist is patient, he may watch them for hours and find that they go on talking to one another for hours, speaking very, very loudly, so as to be able to hear one another. Their conversation will probably surprise the tourist, for it is conducted on the same high level of sophistry, casuistry and lack of reason that is common in parliaments, in the lectures of philosophers and in the discussions of theologians. Here he will see the art of politics in the germ and he will recognise in these two simple peasants choice material for the manufacture of Prime Ministers, Diplomats and Jesuits. And he will notice, by looking from the peasants to the land, that their power of nonsensical argument is so great that it has charmed the very weeds of the earth, which have sprung up in myriads to listen. The hedges, ditches and houses round about are dishevelled with riotous amusement, listening to this discussion and the whole countryside resembles some drunken debauch, by the unkempt posture in which it is sprawling, while the words fly back and forth from one peasant to another and the plough and the spade, stuck idly in the earth,

Three

with their metal shining in the sunlight, represent the dangers of war that may follow on a disagreement between the two talkers. If the tourist waits until evening, he will see the two peasants go to their village. After supper the whole village gathers and carries on the conversation until near midnight, perhaps at crossroads, perhaps in a public house, perhaps in the house of some old bachelor. Then, utterly exhausted with conversation, they all go to bed.

It is this passion for conversation that makes our politics so amusing and interesting; for once a man finds himself able to speak well, nothing can prevent him from seeking an audience! A platform. A kingdom for a platform! This mania for finding a platform first leads the peasant into opening a little shop, where he can talk all day from behind a counter. He can bang the counter and pretend that it is the rostrum of a public house and as his customers come and go, he gets that insight into human character which is necessary for the politician. Thus the tourist will be surprised, as he travels around the country, to see countless numbers of hucksters' shops, and he will very probably come to the conclusion that Ireland should be called the island of hucksters, just as Napoleon called the English a nation of shopkeepers. But he will be mistaken if he thinks that the hucksters are hucksters through pure love of huckstering. They are merely hucksters through love of conversation and of politics, to which huckstering is an apprenticeship. All hucksters, however, are not called to politics. Some of them make the mistake of going immediately into the political battlefield by standing for some petty local election and getting stuck there. The subtle hucksters wait until they can change their huckster's shop into a public house. Then they are at the door of higher politics. Here again the tourist must be warned about these public houses. But hold ... We must deal separately with the public house and the publicans.

The huckstering peasants supply the rank and file of politicians. The leaders and the officials come from the middle classes. The legal profession supplies most of them. The tourist may have been a little surprised and somewhat offended that I did not undertake to examine the legal profession in this country, but he must now understand that I did not do so because the legal profession here is so soaked in politics that it is impossible to make it stand on its own feet and submit to being examined. Let them be examined as politicians. Doctors and strong farmers and labour leaders also act as political leaders, but in lesser quantities. Pig jobbers, cattle men and geniuses without any economic label have been known to come forward on occasions, but the pig jobbers and cattle men proved too barbarous even for our none too polite public life and the geniuses were exterminated as soon as it became known that they were geniuses. In the background of course are the priests, who hold the scales of judgment and decide what politicians are to be supported or condemned. But in this study the priests must play second fiddle.

However in studying the character of the politicians it must be remembered that it was the priests who

Three

moulded them, by regulating their education. And as we have seen that the priests regard the state as an enemy to be exploited, it is only natural that our politicians do likewise. Thus, although patriotism is held in greater esteem in this country than in any other country in the world, there is no other country in the world where patriotism is less in evidence among politicians and among the general mass of the community. For patriotism and the state are so closely allied that love of one is necessarily love of the other. And if any man considers the state an enemy and an institution to be exploited, it follows naturally that he is no patriot. Thus the amazed tourist will see that it is very fashionable for Irish politicians who are not in the government to denounce the government and then when they get into the government it is equally fashionable for them to use the powers of government for the purpose of robbing the country.

In point of fact, as a result of clerical education, the whole population suffers from an extraordinary psychological disease and the politicians, being that portion of the population that finds greater expression for its energies, suffer from this disease to an extraordinary degree. This disease is the attempt to unite mysticism with reality. It is all very well in religious matters to start off by saying that God is a mystery and then to prove his existence by logic, because after all God is a hypothesis and his hypothetical existence cannot interfere with the growth of crops or with the rainfall. Further, the Jesuits who make it their business to discuss the status of God are so clever with words and are so well trained in the matter of juggling with words that this dangerous business has no evil effect on them; at least so far as the public can see, although they may very well hide those that break under the strain and become jabbering idiots. But politics, or the business of managing the state, is altogether different from the business of regulating the affairs of the Heavenly World. And nothing concerned with the state should be a mystery or hypothetical.

The disease of which I have spoken manifests itself among our politicians principally in the belief that Ireland is a living being; a woman in fact. This woman is claimed by them to be a very beautiful creature and very unfortunate and they consider themselves in duty bound to succour her. They love her under different names and it appears that the wench has a very great number of aliases; in other words that she has changed her lovers more often than she should if she wanted to lead a quiet life. At one moment she is Caitlín Ní Houliháin, at another Róisín Dubh, at another The Old Woman of Beara. She changes her name to suit the particular character of the politician that courts her.

Having started with the hypothesis that Ireland is a woman, the politicians conduct themselves exactly like suitors. They use every means, fair and foul, to win possession of the woman's body, for all is fair in love and war. When they have obtained possession of her body, they remember suddenly that they are not the first by any means who have had that pleasure and in jealous rage they loot her of all her trinkets and then desert her. Their successors, very probably finding her

Three

penniless and in rags, call her the old hag of Beara. They in turn pull out her teeth, cut her about the face and force her to go and beg for them, from her children in the United States of America. No politician seriously thinks of making a decent home for the woman, of educating the children she has had by former lovers or of trying to cure her of her naughty ways; which they might very well succeed in doing if they treated her kindly and remained faithful to her. They are doubtless prevented from adopting this latter humane course by the teaching of the priests, who, as we have seen, regard women and the amorous pleasure of intercourse with them as the source of all evil.

This must be clearly borne in mind by the tourist if he ever hopes to understand Irish politics and if he does not understand them he cannot properly enjoy them. And he must further understand that since the priests regard the salvation of the human soul of much greater importance than the feeding, cleansing and civilising of the human body and the human mind, so do the politicians regard the soul of the nation as of greater consequence than the mere welfare of the nation's citizens. Like true libertines they preach sermons to their lady between embraces. And even, when by their greed and stupidity they have reduced the woman to starvation, they point with a proud finger at other wealthy countries, where politicians are not mystical and say that Holy Ireland is above such coarse ambitions as wealth, culture, bathrooms, tooth brushes and machinery.

However, I must say that when our politicians attain

power they show signs of trying to become realistic and they seem to sneer at mysticism; but the priests are there in the background and it is so far impossible to do anything really sensible while the priests stand threatening in the background. Because even though the politicians discover that Ireland's body is more important than her soul, they also know that if they act on that discovery the priests are going to join the opposition and throw them out. So the politicians who form the government are always forced to be cynical ruffians and to speak in divers tongues and to conduct the business of the state like a man playing many instruments simultaneously. As it were, they have the deafening drum of mysticism tied to their chest and the cymbals of patriotism strapped to their elbows, while other instruments are tied to their toes and to their hands and a penny whistle is held between their teeth. By the discordant roar of these many instruments everybody is confused and the politicians try to play to every sort of an audience.

Of course the tourist will want facts. He will principally want to know why taxation is so high, why Dublin is the most expensive city in Europe, why Irish whiskey is dearer in Ireland than it is in England, why Irish roads are bad for motorists compared to English roads. He will accuse the politicians of causing all this expense and inconvenience to the tourist. He may also say that if the politicians were more concerned with their proper business than with the soul of Ireland they would see to it that the art of cookery was taught in the schools, so that Irish hotels and restaurants might be

Three

able to feed the tourist in a civilised manner. I admit all that, but I beg of the tourist to remember that people who seek the spectacle of vice must pay extra. High taxes, bad food, bad roads, expensive whiskey and slow trains might be an inconvenience without recompense in a dull country like Switzerland, but in Ireland the pleasure to be had from politics makes one forget all the drawbacks.

Is there any tourist in the whole world of such dull wit as not to be moved to an ecstasy of delight by the spectacle of a whole nation arguing for a number of years about the nature of an oath? In most countries wars are waged over intelligible things like territory, money and real estate, but our politicians waged a civil war over the wording of an oath. Even after the war had been finished, they still went on arguing. The argument has now ceased and the result of the whole business is that the position is exactly what it was before the war and the argument. Nobody knows yet what is an oath and which oath of the oaths about which the war was waged is the better oath. Indeed, as a result of the war and the argument the people have come to the conclusion that an oath is worth very little, and they abuse it on every manner of occasion to the great detriment of the state. The tourist will remember the casuistry of the two peasants he heard talking in the fields, by the idle ploughs. He will also remember that famous assembly of clergy that argued for a long time about the possession by woman of an immortal soul. Then he will understand how an extremely intelligent people like ourselves could argue for years about an oath. I know he'll find it amusing, for the tourist in matters like this is a rascal without conscience. Just as people at a theatre never paused in their laughter to see the human suffering behind the clown's grin, so the laughing tourist will not trouble to see the hunger and misery in the hollow cheeks and sunken eyes of our people, while our politicians are arguing and laying waste the country because of an oath.

However, let the tourist have his day. I feel it is my duty, as a man who has a sense of the dignity of his country, to let the tourist have as much amusement as possible in return for all the mulcting from which he suffers. Just as he got in touch with the parish priest, he must now get in touch with the politician. In this case he will not go to a country district. There he would only get small fry like county councillors and the secretaries of branches of political parties and mysterious youths who are members of mysterious organisations, known only to the police. Dublin is the hunting ground in this instance. Dublin is the seat of government. It is headquarters of the principle banks. The treasury is there. The important politicians, therefore, never go very far away from it. For as the honey bee settles on the honeyed flower, so does the politician settle near the money.

In this instance, it is absolutely no use for the tourist to go up to a politician and make him a donation of five or ten pounds for his cause. The tourist must pose as somebody whom the politician thinks of importance. If he wants to go among the government politicians he should pose as a foreign capitalist who has money to

Three

invest in the country. Among the opposition, who are at present the party known as Fianna Fail, he should pose as an American of Irish descent, who is fairly well off for an American and wants to start a newspaper in Ireland on strictly national lines. In this case he should stress the importance of bringing home to the government the blame for having started the Civil War, as that seems to be the principal plank in the programme of the opposition. If he wants to approach the labour leaders, he should stay at his hotel and spare himself the trouble, because they are dull and identical with labour leaders in his own country. If he wants to approach the revolutionary groups, he should pose as having come from Russia.

Among the government politicians, he should be extremely tactful, and point out to each that all the others are incompetent and owe their existence in political life solely to the man to whom he is talking. In return for this just remark, the politician will unbosom his inmost soul to the tourist, who is posing as a capitalist. He will point out that of course he, the politician, is of different stuff from all the other politicians but that he is hampered in his efforts to place the country on its feet by the poor material with which he has to work. He will tell the tourist that the peasants are hopeless. The opposition is appealing to the greed and ignorance of the peasants and for this reason, in order to counter the opposition, the government must do likewise. In the same manner, he will tell the tourist that in order to counter the opposition, the government has to toy with the idea of resurrecting the Irish language, which is the

49

chief plank in the opposition platform, next to proving that the government was responsible for the Civil War. This toying with the language, he will say, wastes a lot of time and energy, but it is going to be gradually sidetracked and will eventually die out, as soon as the last native speaker has emigrated to America; because the politician will be careful to point out, as a phenomenon discovered by a new statistical system invented by the government, that it is impossible to prevent native speakers from emigrating to America, for the supposed reason that they feel more at home in that country than in Ireland and have more relatives there. Personally, I doubt this. I am rather inclined to believe that the reason why it is impossible to keep Irish speakers in Ireland is that since they live on doles from their relatives in America they go over to that country in order to be nearer their source of revenue. But the politician will point out to the supposed capitalist that the government's policy of reviving the language and cutting the ground from under the feet of the opposition is in no wise hampered by the disappearance of the native speakers. The government have hired a few men in Dublin to manufacture Irish words according as they are needed.

When he hears that the tourist is a capitalist who has got money to invest, the politician will be very glad indeed, because he has got one or more relatives who are quite willing to be directors and he himself might be willing to have some interest in the business; because he never knows when he may lose office and while he is in office he must feather his nest, since it is

Three

more than likely that he had no nest before he came into office. He is quite ready to get the state to subsidise the tourist's projected industry, because, as we have seen before, no politician in this country considers the state in any other light than as an institution to be exploited. He will treat the tourist to a dinner or two. He will likely take him to a race meeting and tip him a few winners. He will take him to a dance and to a party, where the tourist may meet other notabilities and many women, without any very great attraction, who are ready to lionise him because he is a foreigner.

On the other hand, if the tourist prefers to meet a politician of the opposition camp, he must refrain from meeting a politician of the government camp, because he will be considered an enemy of the country by the opposition if he is seen in the company of one of the government. I must say that on second thoughts I don't advise the tourist to mix with the politicians of the opposition. Not being in office, they are poor, and being poor, they are more in the power of the national characteristic virtue of Puritanism, which fattens on empty pockets. They will oppress the tourist with rambling accounts of all the murders committed by members of the government, of the corruption practised by all branches of the Civil Service, of the inefficiency of the police and with lamentations on the dreadful state of the country. I must warn the tourist not to pay much heed to these statements. Our politicians are inept and perhaps a trifle corrupt, like all politicians, but as a race we are not murderously inclined, and even the members of the government are quite harmless fellows. And I must say that our police are the most efficient force in Europe. So let the tourist sleep quietly in his bed. In fact, he may take the statements of the opposition as a lot of stuff and nonsense, just as he would take the statements of any jealous lover who is moaning on the doorstep of his mistress, while his rival is within making a merry noise with champagne glasses and reclining in boudoirs, whence gentle sounds ensue, suggestive of kisses.

But it would pay the tourist to make the acquaintance of the revolutionary groups. As I stated already, he might claim to have come from Russia or some other country that is reputed by the newspapers to have gold to throw about for the purpose of starting revolutions. Why Russia has got the reputation of having gold to scatter broadcast for this purpose I know not, because she is poorer than our country, and goodness knows we are poor enough. But she has that reputation, just as in England we have the reputation of being violent, whereas ours is the most peaceful country in Europe, and we are guilty of violence only in our minds and on our tongues. The tourist must understand this, when he comes in contact with our revolutionary groups. Their passwords, their secret movements and their hair-raising programmes must be taken with a smile because they mean nothing of it. Here again he will see the result of the priestly culture of the art of conversation, for the activities of these groups never lead any further than conversation, unless it be some utterly purposeless act committed by what Dostoievsky called the 'Contemplatives': those fellows who meditate for

Three

years and then suddenly, for no apparent reason, burn a house, murder a man, or go on a pilgrimage to Lourdes or Jerusalem. Of revolutionary groups, with constructive programmes and with leaders that are clear-thinking and ambitious men, the tourist will see no sign here. Our educational system does not provide for them. Yet there is no country in the world where a Cromwell or a Lenin is more needed.

Let the tourist then be warned against Irish politics and let him have no more truck with Irish politics than he would have with Irish fairies. We have had many instances in the last and the present generations of foreigners coming here as simple tourists and staying here in the role of patriots who want to free the country. But their efforts seem to have resulted in giving us more politicians, whereas if the country is really to be freed, it should be freed from priests, politicians, ignorance and various other diseases. The love of woman in the flesh may lead man to grave excesses. But the love of a mystical woman like Caitlín Ní Houliháin does untold harm. For that reason, let all foreigners keep a grip on their purses and on their minds, lest they be induced by the whispering winds that float about our beautiful mountains to see spirits in the air. There is where, I am told, Irish mystical patriotism originates. The country needs real patriotism badly, and it oozes in red blood from rich beefsteak, just as it does in England and in other prosperous countries. If the tourist wants to benefit his children who may come as tourists to Ireland, he should mock and jeer at our mysticism until he shames us out of it. Then we may learn to cook him a good meal and not try to use him as our solitary source of real revenue. For if our politics progress as they are at present, our whole population will shortly be receiving a pension from the state and there will be no other means of levying the revenue to pay this common pension than by mulcting tourists. This is true. The present government have pensioned a great number. The opposition, if they come into power, are likely to pension as many more. Add to that the number of politicians who do no useful work. Add to that all priests who do no useful work. Add the lawyers who do no useful work. Add to that the police, the army and the civil services, who do not produce wealth. Add the shopkeepers who do not produce wealth but merely distribute it. There remain only the peasants and Guinness's brewery and a few industries that are rapidly dying out. The peasants are going to America as rapidly as they can. Those that remain are living on the old age pensions of their fathers and mothers, and cursing the government for not providing them with sufficient doles. Nobody thinks of the solution of the problem of this universal poverty and universal discussion.

What is it?

~ *Four* ~

What should be the attitude of the tourist towards the publicans? Righteous fury and nothing less. If any man in Ireland robs the tourist it is the publican. He robs him in every way that it is conceivable to rob a tourist. Here it must be understood that I refuse to consider the case of those tourists who are inhuman teetotallers. For any tourist who refuses to recognise that the most beneficent products of human labour are the grape, the hop and the ear of barley is a low ruffian and only fit to be incarcerated in some remote part of Texas, where throats are as dry as the climate and the lack of invigorating stimulants produces a mania called Fundamentalism; which is presumably a disease first discovered by Dr Rabelais, for he was always referring to the falling of that part of the human anatomy in dire stress. I cannot conceive of a tourist going on a tour anywhere, unless it be for the purpose of drinking at leisure. Although not a great drinker myself, because of poverty and constitutional disability, I have noticed, with envy, that when my own countrymen go on a little tour anywhere, be it to a distant race meeting or a football match, or to see a ruin, or to attend a congress, or a political meeting, or a funeral, or a wedding — in other words, when a party of my countrymen set out anywhere for any purpose beyond the three-mile limit of their wives and families, their tour becomes a drinking bout and they forget the purpose of their tour, if it had any purpose other than an excuse to get away beyond the three-mile limit of their wives and families. This tour, or even the sight of it, seems to me to be the most glorious sort of human amusement, for it combines all the human concepts of happiness, motion, leisure, company, freedom from observation, intoxication and, mayhap, the sweets of love sucked by the way. In this way, when I see a charabanc laden with Dublin dock labourers coming out from the city and heading for the country, en route no doubt to make a pious pilgrimage to St Kevin's bed at Glendalough, I make a mental bet that they'll never get farther than Tallon's of Enniskerry. Or if they do pass Tallon's, will they pass Talty's of Kilmacanogue? Or perhaps they will pass Talty's and climb the Sugar Loaf as far as the Mountain Tavern? And even farther than that ... But it's certain they'll never go beyond Roundwood. For even if en route they drink dry the three public houses I have mentioned, Roundwood will be well to floor them. Then delirious with happiness and perhaps with a multitude of bandages on their skulls they return to Dublin, roaring out bawdy songs. Ah! These are sights that might still cheer Oisín, the son of Fionn, if he returned to the country from the Land of Youth on his old white steeplechasing nag. But if he saw

Four

a party of dry Americans on the same tour and mistook them for Irish people, I'm afraid he'd lay waste the whole countryside as far as the Yellow House at Rathfarnham. There no doubt he'd be so thirsty after the slaughter that the good proprietor of that famous pub could make him blind drunk and save the city from sacking.

This little rambling discourse was undertaken with the express purpose of showing the tourist that the glorious instinct for revelry is still alive in our country and that is indeed a great tribute to our people, considering the monstrous hindrances that are placed in the way of drinking and revelry by the publicans. The tourist, if he is a drinking man, will have often heard it said of some worthy fellow that he would drink whiskey out of a sewer. Well, that man that would drink whiskey out of a sewer would probably not notice that the average Irish public house is different from a decent tavern in any other country. But he would be the only one. No decent tourist will fail to notice that the average Irish public house is a melancholy and often foul-smelling hut, where a dour-visaged individual stands behind a counter and looks at his customer with a forbidding glance. Very often, on the counter, beside the glass that is pushed towards him, the tourist will see a great piece of salty American bacon, or a little sack of flour on which somebody has spilled some sugar or some hayseed. On the floor, among the dried expectoration of all the customers that have visited the place for twenty years, he'll see new and ancient refuse of all sorts, and in the corner perhaps he may see an old bitch of a dog that has given birth to pups on a litter of straw. He'll swallow his whiskey and feel a pang of terror as it goes down his throat and he'll rush out into the open air wondering whether water or poison has made the whiskey taste different. I can assure him that both guesses are right. Or if he drank the wine of the country, Guinness's black beer in bottle, he will wonder to an equal degree now such a famous drink can taste so sour, until he chances to read in the newspapers the numerous public apologies that are offered to the firm of Guinness by the publicans that have sold a mixture of bog water and boot blacking as stout. If the tourist is cycling, walking, motoring or riding in remote places and he gets hungry in the course of the journey of one hundred miles or so from one good hotel to another, he may hope to get a meal at a public house. He may have read Dickens, who knew so well how to describe the pleasure of arrival at an inn and of getting the smell of roast beef or of chicken broth. Alas! Tea, bread of a kind and salt mixed with a little American bacon is the only food he can find. And let him not ask for this food in a public house. As we say, 'they'll look sideways at ye.' And this look will be for the purpose of seeing which part of your anatomy is the most susceptible to a good kick. For it must be known that an Irish publican does not believe that a customer should eat. He should only drink. Food is troublesome to cook and the profit is not more, at the highest, than one hundred per cent. But drink costs very little trouble to serve in a glass that has not been cleaned very well, and the profit is anything up to a thousand per cent.

My tourist is undoubtedly a civilised man, a man who is aware of the customs prevalent among human

Four

beings during the great ages of history. And he will know that eating and drinking are the foundation stones of all true culture. How do people eat? How do they drink? Answer me these two questions, and I will answer and tell you whether these people in question are great, civilised and cultured, or whether they are just barbarous louts. During the reign of Queen Elizabeth in England, and again in the eighteenth century, the English ate and drank like Gods. For who has not envied the age when one could see with Shakespeare a 'fair belly with fat capon lined'? In France and over the Continent, the reigns of Francis I and of Charles V and of the great pope that arrived in Rome with a horde of mistresses synchronised with an age when feasting and drinking were regal, and as a result of this good feeding and great drinking, art, culture, beauty and genius flourished in abundance. The tourist will know this, and when he sees his meal of bread, tea and salty American bacon set before him in a dusky, murky room, full of photographs of popes and priests and patriots, he'll rush forth and execrate the name of Ireland. For here, food or drink does not receive that respect that is owed them, considering their divine purpose in preparing the human body and the human mind for the fulfilment of human greatness. Here one must eat like a hermit in the desert, in order that the parish priest may have abundance for his table. Here one must drink, standing up like a cab-horse at a drinking trough, black beverages that remind us of the death that is the common destiny of us all. And one must drink quickly, on an empty stomach, drink after drink, diluted and weakened, so that the publican may rake in quickly, with little labour, enough money to make his sons priests, doctors, lawyers and politicians, and then to build a new church or repair an old one, as a duty to God and to save his immortal soul in payment for all the robbery he has committed.

There should be no calling more noble than that of the country publican. No calling, to my mind, has contributed more to the development of civilisation. For at the village inn, the village wits are sharpened, and the village genius is fanned into flame by the fumes of good liquor and the competition and adulation of other minds. There the pleasure and profit of association is discovered, and it may very well have happened that it was at an inn that the first city was planned, the first theatre, the first song. There new food is tested, being brought hither by some traveller and brought to the households by husbands who urge their wives to cook similar dishes. There that silence and introspection which leads to insanity is driven from the mind of the peasant by the laughter of his fellows and the cheerful gleam of polished pewter and the cheerful roar of great inn fires in winter. There thought of passion springs into the heart of youth, fanned by wine and spirits, and the race is perpetuated by means of the courage and energy generated in the munificent inn. The damsel who seemed to stand walled within her skirts as within a fortress stands nude and beseeching and beautiful before the mind of the village gallant who staggers from the good inn with vine leaves in his hair. And the fat, laughing publican, with bare arms

Four

folded on his capacious belly, is the god of all pleasure and of all good to his customers. No matter how remote from the city and from the centre of civilisation, there in the inn, the great fights, the great races, the great battles, the great acts of heroism are recounted and commented upon, and they live again and are enacted amidst shouts and bravos and bursts of laughter on the bar-room floor, while the amber-coloured beer and the gleaming wine and the sly whiskey are poured from glass and pewter measure into wide-open throats. No priestly confessional can wash away sin as effectually as the bar-room can wash away the cares and miseries of existence and within its precincts the devils of sorrow and death cannot find service, no matter how loud they may shout. For they are forgotten, despised, unknown. Forsooth, there is the land of youth.

I speak of good inns and of merry publicans, men who are conscious of their great position in society and of their duty to their fellow men. But of Irish publicans and of Irish public houses the exact opposite must be told. There is no darker stain on our national honour than our public houses. And I am firmly convinced that the cause of this is the close association between the publicans and the priests. For the publicans are, as a general rule, the fathers of our priests, and the perverted conception of the universe and of man's mission on this earth taught by the priests leads the publicans into those evil ways of which I have spoken. Old Job, that most disreputable of Jews, scraping his filthy sores on a dunghill instead of going to a doctor, seems to be the patron saint of Irish publicans; but our publicans have apparently discovered more about the habits of Job than has been disclosed in the Bible, for, according to the publicans, he also had a fair-sized treasure hidden in the dunghill, and that is why he was sitting there and why he could not go to a doctor and put it in danger of being stolen.

Now that I have told the tourist the truth about the Irish publican, it is as well to remind him that there are a few honourable exceptions. There are a few manly fellows that struggle against the tide of dirt, corruption and melancholy, and my friend, Mr Byrne of Duke Street, Dublin, must understand that anything I have said to the detriment of Irish public houses has positively no reference to his excellent house. There is a house where one may find good company and good liquor at any hour of the day or night, and a good host into the bargain. There are others, scattered about the country, but they are very few, and it would pay the government to draw up a list of good public houses and thus save the honour of the country. But it is too much to expect of any government. The publicans are so powerful here, almost as powerful as the priests, that it would be suicidal for any government, no matter how powerful, to gainsay them. There has been an effort to limit their number, but it is still difficult to find a small village where there are less than ten. The numbers of these public houses would lead one to suppose that we are a nation of drunkards, and yet we drink less than any nation in Europe. The cost of the drink consumed in our country is very great, but that is no proof that we drink a lot. We simply cannot afford it. The price is too high.

~ Five ~

The tourist must pity and admire the peasants. He may also despise them, because any man that is deserving of pity is also deserving of contempt. But it is only an Irish peasant that can merit at one and the same time both contempt and admiration. Of course the opinions of a tourist are worth very little, as he judges everything from a purely selfish and material point of view. Like George Moore, confronted with the Venus de Milo, he only thinks of writing his name in pencil on the statue's rump. His attitude to the Irish peasant will be only merely of curiosity, and he will carry in his brain all that he has ever heard of the Irish peasant, and he will be pleased if the peasant is like what he has heard and displeased if he is different.

The tourist may take it for granted at once that the Irish peasant is quite different from what he has been painted. English writers and historians have claimed him to be a good-natured buffoon, no doubt with the desire that he might become one and remain one and remaining one after having become one, go on paying rents and living in huts and tipping his hat to officials, and if he saw an Englishman fouling the outer wall of his cabin, asking him courteously to do a like service, with greater comfort, to the inner walls. Such is the peasant of a conquered country, and, indeed, of all countries where the feudal system prevails and the lords have to use field glasses when trying to pick out a peasant from among their dogs. But in my own generation, the Irish peasant has become quite a different character. He is in process of transformation, and goodness only knows where he may get to and what he may become. Personally, I like him, and he is the only natural type of human being in this country that I consider an honour to the country and to mankind. As he forms ninety per cent of the community, it will be seen that I consider the Irish race a very fine race. But, like a mangy dog, the peasant needs a good and continuous treatment with some stringent sort of medicine in order to rid him of all the parasites I have named in preceding chapters.

Of course the parasites do not wish him to clean himself, and the literary hirelings of the parasites are even more fanatical than the English Government was formerly in trying to persuade the Irish peasant that he is a harmless idiot and that he should remain one. In a later chapter I propose to deal with those literary hirelings that still dishonour our country by trying to persuade us that the peasant is a babbling child of God, who is innocent of all ambition, ignorant of guile, midway between heaven and earth, enveloped in a cloud of mystical adoration of the priests and of Caitlín

Five

Ní Houliháin, the Raparee with a pike in his thatch, the Croppy Boy confessing his sins on his way to the scaffold to suffer a patriotic martyrdom, a violent primitive who runs wild, naked and raving mad, once the gentle hand of the priest is raised from his back, a holy, sexless ascetic whose loins never cry out for the pleasure of love, a quantity as fixed and unchangeable as the infallibility of the Pope. If a peasant is indeed such a fellow, then there is no hope for the race, and I am wrong in thinking that our race has a great future, and that out of the loins of our washed peasantry is going to spring a tribe of human beings that is going to do honour to mankind.

No doubt all peasants in all countries are used by frantic writers to form the basis of some idealistic concept of the universe or the basis for a jingoistic patriotism. Even the English yokel, whom I know personally to have no more than sixty words or so in his vocabulary, is always referred to as a sturdy yeoman and the material out of which English greatness is built, the backbone of the country, and a great deal of other rubbish. Of course, the truth about the greatness of the English is that they save all except the most stupid from the horrors of a peasant life and use these most stupid as serfs and cannon fodder. No responsible newspaper will allow an English writer to blether about the superior virtues of a peasant life as compared to that of a town life, or that the peasant is the superior of the townsman. From the casual observations that I have made in England, both in the cities and in the rural districts, it seems to me that the London cockney, when well fed and fairly well informed, is the superior in every way of any peasant in any country, physically, morally and mentally.

Our writers, who are paid to preach the righteousness and the divine mission of the priests, exalt the peasants by ascribing to them virtues that demoralise and degrade them, just because our towns are a disgrace to civilisation and morality, and the Grace of God, which must result from such numbers of priests, must fall among the peasants since it does not fall among the townspeople. On the other hand, while I do not ascribe to our peasants in their present state any exalted qualities of civilisation and culture, I see in them the germs of future greatness.

Peasants, as compared to civilised human beings, are children. All civilised races have begun by scraping the earth, and it is only when they stop scraping the earth and build cities that they grow up and become responsible, thoughtful citizens, that are not surprised at natural phenomena and that struggle to obtain mastery over nature by the construction of machinery, by the investigation of unknown places on the earth and in the firmament, by the destruction of old Gods and by the formation of new ones, by the development of the human mind through intricate processes of thought, by a continual accumulation of knowledge, and by learning to offer to culture and to art the respect that was formerly given to spooks and fetishes by savage men and peasants.

As in the life of the individual, childhood is the age where the brute instincts hold sway over the undeveloped

Five

mind, so in the life of the human species the peasant stage is that in which man is also under the control of the brute instincts. The word in this instance is divorced from its usual meaning. For peasants and children have many endearing qualities. Their laughter for instance, the ease with which they amuse themselves, their simplicity, their lack of vulgarity, that dreadful quality which seems impossible to disassociate from the struggle to pass from a peasant life to that of an educated person and which it is impossible to analyse excepting by adding to it the word bourgeois. The peasant has also another quality which makes him very charming, and that is his uniformity with nature. Seeing him with a cow, his slow gait and his downcast head strike no jarring note. Even his jaws moving slowly as they chew a wisp of straw move in unison with those of the cow that is chewing her cud. He responds to the seasons like a bird or beast, clothing himself heavily or lightly, ploughing, reaping, sowing, or hiding in his hut, according as the cold or heat of nature bids him. He reproduces his kind methodically, without any concept of romantic love, and he dies practically without effort, since his imagination is not strong enough to torment him with visions.

But on the other hand, his life is as miserable as that of a child, and he is really as cruel as a child and as selfish and as obstinate. He has all the horrible qualities of the child. Just as the child is a menace to the household, so is the peasant a menace to society and to good government.

And as nothing is more pitiable than a father with a

score of children, so is the state, in which ninety per cent of the citizens are peasants. The father with twenty children is haggard, with furtive eyes and furrowed forehead. He is threadbare. He is penniless. He has to shun the companionship of his fellow men. Because of the dread menace of hunger in his house, he is narrow minded and bigoted, a hater of all progress, a toady to his superiors and a violent hater of all pleasure and leisure, since he has none himself. His house is like a bedlam, and no guest cares to enter the place, for the number of the children has rendered it impossible for the father to control them or teach them manners. They grow up wild and in a natural state, and it's odds on their burning his house for their amusement, or cutting him into small portions and drowning him in a river like a cat, or robbing him of all he possesses and turning him out of doors. Terrified by their numbers, he uses all sorts of subterfuges in the hope of keeping them within bounds, and he is afraid to give them any decent sort of education, which would develop their natural traits along decent lines, lest they discover his failings and despise him.

In the same way, a state that has a multitude of peasants has to spend a great portion of its time using as many tricks and subterfuges as a conjuror. And especially a state like ours, that is based on the mystical power of priests and extraordinary politicians, has to resort to diverse evil tricks for keeping the peasants in their state of ignorance and helplessness. For nothing makes a man more cunning than hunger and adversity. And our politicians, being the curious sort of people

Five

that they are, under the impression that their business is to rob the state and not to civilise the country, just try to keep the peasants quiet instead of trying to educate them.

There are countries like France where the peasant is a valuable economic asset to the state. But in our country, a great number of the peasants are of absolutely no value to the state. A great number of them are a part of the national debt. Not only do they not produce a surplus of wealth, but they do not produce enough to feed themselves. For this they blame the government. Their sole capital seems to be a capacity for producing children. They manage to rear these children somehow or other and send them to the United States, where the children go to work and feed their parents. Those peasants who are not clever enough to send their children to the United States in time develop famines and portion off some of their number to die of hunger. Then there is a national collection and the proceeds of this charity is used to send the children of the remaining peasants to the United States, whence they send home money to feed their parents. Thus the twin ambitions of a great portion of our peasants are to send their children to the United States and to go to Heaven after death. The state makes no effort to change these ambitions, for it obvious that if the peasants changed their minds and stayed at home, their numbers would become so great that they would get out of control and murder their father the state.

Of those peasants that do produce wealth an almost similar story has to be told. Instead of producing children in great numbers they produce cattle, which they sell in England. This money, resulting from the sale of cattle, might be of use to the country if it were not used in the manufacture of publicans, lawyers, priests and politicians. Thus, no matter how you look at the peasant, he is not an economic asset. He is merely the mainstay of the extraordinary and unstable state of society prevalent here at present. And it seems to me most unfair that the tourist should be called upon to pay for all this; for now, having seen that the peasants, upon whom we depended so far, produce nothing of the real revenue of the country, there remain only the tourist and Guinness's Brewery to pay the piper. Where else would it come from? Answer me that. There is no Manna nowadays, and even if there were, no Jewish food would fall in this priest-ridden country, so hostile to Jews.

Another extraordinary arrangement in this country is responsible for the uselessness of the peasants as a national asset. That is the distribution of the land. Practically all the rich land of Ireland is lying idle and uninhabited in the centre of the country, while the great bulk of the peasants live on the rocky coasts and among the rocky mountains. This is quite true, although the tourist may want to see it before he believes it. I can explain it in no other way than by supposing that the priests have ordained it so; finding it easier to send souls to Heaven from rocky, barren land, where life is miserable and fasting is easy, than from rich juicy land, where life is comfortable and fasting difficult. That may not be the case, really, but there is a plausibility about it

Five

which is worth consideration. Whatever is the explanation, the tourist should look into the matter, for it concerns him very gravely. While the peasants, who are, after all, the workmen that supply the tourist's table, live on rocky land, the tourist will be without vegetables.

The Irish peasant lives on tea, bread, potatoes and sometimes American bacon, though that is a delicacy which is only tasted by the richer peasants. He does not object to cabbages, which he cultivates occasionally, but he abhors all other vegetables. Turnips and mangolds he cultivates for his cattle, and he sometimes eats a turnip. But he considers that lettuces, carrots, radishes, parsnips, peas, beans, spinach and cress are only food for animals. And indeed he would not risk giving them to his cow. He rarely drinks, for he rarely has money to buy drink. Only on fair days, when he has sold cattle or pigs and has received luck penny from the buyer, does he go into a public house and, standing at the counter, rapidly drinks, one after the other, from six to fourteen pints of porter. Then he is dragged home by his wife, singing or weeping, according to his temperament, to another long period of abstinence. He very rarely dances, sings or laughs, as there does not seem to be anything to gain by these amusements and perhaps if the gombeen man caught him at either pastime there might be trouble.

For the tourist must understand, finally and definitely, that the pivot of Irish life is not even the peasant, although we had hopes in that direction, but the gombeen man. What is a gombeen man? He is the vice of usury. He is not really an occupation, because he appears under many different guises, and as a rule under many different guises simultaneously. But as a general description it suffices to describe him as the man for whom the peasant works.

We have seen that the peasant is exploited by the priests and by the politicians, but the greatest exploitation is that done by the gombeen man. It works out this way. A young peasant couple get married. As a rule their marriage portion is exhausted by the marriage ceremonies, the priest's fees and the furnishing of the home. If the husband had little drinking bills, these bills absorb whatever is left of the money brought in by the wife. The husband is sure to have brought in no money, as it required the expenditure of whatever money he had to summon up courage to get married. Finding themselves without money, they have to go to the local shopkeeper for credit until their pigs are fit for sale or until the next cattle fair arrives. The shopkeeper accepts their stock as a sort of pledge. When they sell their stock they may have just enough to pay off the debt and begin again on credit. The shopkeeper is not particularly anxious to have them pay off all the debt at any time. He advises them generously to keep a little for the priest or for the current political movement to save the country. For the more they get into debt the better it is for the shopkeeper. The shopkeeper knows the value of their land and he will give them credit until they have mortgaged in this manner not only their stock and their labour power but real estate to about half its value. Then the shopkeeper may suggest

Five

that they emigrate to Canada or the United States, and in return for their fares he takes their land.

It is only in rare instances that the shopkeeper or gombeen man adopts this latter course. As a rule the peasant couple go on all their lives living on credit, producing cattle and pigs in order to pay off their debt to the gombeen man, and they never succeed in paying it. Even when they rear large numbers of children and send them to America, they still go on paying the debt with the money that is sent home by the children. One often sees, in remote parts of the country, a lonely old couple, on the brink of the grave, decrepit, twisted about the body, bent double, with dead minds and lips that are continually mumbling, but with a proud gleam of happiness in their eyes. These are happy peasants. They have at last paid their debts and they are living in peace on the old age pension. Their children have fled to America. One perhaps has taken the land and has begun the torture of producing another family and living on credit. But the old couple are secure with the old age pension. This is a rare sight, but it is worth seeing, and the tourist should hunt about until he sees it. But he must make sure. For many old couples of that sort are not happy. The son who has got the land very often takes the old-age pension off his parents and uses it to pay *his* debt to the gombeen man. I have seen horrifying scenes, where the son pursues the old father and tears the pension out of his palm. I have seen the old father resist, with tears and curses, and I have seen the son push him brutally to the ground and even kick him and call him horrible names.

And then I have seen the old fellow, robbed of his pension, go about the village begging for tobacco. Such is the rapacity of the gombeen man, that it drives the peasant to commit all manner of atrocities, even the robbery of an old father.

I have also seen a mother take off her flannel skirt in winter and rip it open and sell the cloth to the gombeen man in order to feed her children. And the gombeen man gave her one-third the price of the good cloth in flour of poor quality. I remember that the same woman died of consumption shortly afterwards, leaving six children; and her husband got three barrels of porter on credit from the publican to bury her properly, using his pigs as pledges. He also borrowed money to pay the priest for saying a mass over her. The last time I saw him, he was a haggard, shifty wretch, and his children were all in consumption and neither the gombeen man nor the publican were paid for the funeral.

I say the tourist may see wonderful sights among the peasants, horrifying ones, and if he is a civilised man, he will be amazed that any society, not to mention the society of saints and scholars, could allow human beings to live in such a manner in their midst; and then prate to the world about these human beings being midway between Heaven and earth, patriots, croppy boys, sexless ascetics, mystic loons. He will see a great horde of stupefied peasants, surrounded on all sides by rapacious rogues that fall upon every little morsel produced by the peasants and tear it to pieces in their ravenous beaks. He will see the decent peasants

Five

becoming fatalists and hopeless wrecks, who wave their hands in despair and say that it is no use to labour or to produce wealth, since all things pass into the pockets of the priests, the gombeen men and the politicians. He will see these decent peasants shiftless, dirty, hungry, without a concept of truth or high morality, subservient, fawning, grovelling, terrified of life and death, eager for revenge, envious of success, fickle in their allegiance, unstable in their resolutions, excitable in temperament; for it is the decent human being who is most easily and surely broken by an overwhelming oppression of this description. He will also see that it is the cunning type of peasant that rises out of this hellish life, using his cunning and rapacity and his shameless indifference to honour and decency for the purpose of making himself into one of the oppressors. It is the cunning and mean peasant who becomes the huckster, the gombeen man, the priest, the politician, and then lives, cannibal-wise, on his own flesh and blood.

The tourist will also see, here and there, a sign and portent of salvation, some brave soul standing up and crying out the gospel of revolt and salvation. These visions are still rare, as rare as the happy old peasants we have seen dying in peace. But they exist and like a white star in the sky at dawn, they are a sign of the morning sun. And it is through the fiery eyes of these rebels that the Irish peasant must really be seen and not through his dirt, his hunger, his apathy and the helpless hands that he waves despairingly at the sky in which he sees no heaven of the blest. These voices crying from the depths of hell shall bring up great forces of revolt, armed with the great wisdom of the damned, and they shall spread over the land and inhabit it with free men and women, free from usurers and soothsayers.